eBay Bookkeeping Made Easy

Contact me at

E-mail: hi@nickvulich.com
Blog: indieauthorstoolbox.com

Amazon Author Page:

- amazon.com/author/nickvulich
- amazon.com/author/nicholasvulich

Why you need to read this book

It's a great feeling when you're selling on eBay and the money keeps rolling in.

I have the eBay app connected to my iPhone and every time the cash register rings, I know I've got another twenty-five bucks in my pocket. Yeah, me!

Too many sellers get so excited about the money rolling in they never bother to add it all up to see if they're making a profit. Not until it's too late, anyway.

To run a successful business you need to make a profit. The more profit you make, the healthier your business is. Unfortunately, too many sellers never stop to look at the big picture. They assume that because the money keeps flowing in, they must be making a profit.

I felt the same way my first year on eBay. I made over fifteen thousand dollars in sales that year, and I naturally assumed I was making money. Every time I turned around there was another check or more cash in the mailbox. I had to be making money. The thing is when I totaled it all up at the end of the year I discovered I actually lost over a thousand dollars.

How could that be?

Simple answer: I spent more money than I took in. The long answer was I purchased too much inventory to support the sales I was making.

Smart business people tie their spending to their cash flow. If they project $10,000 in sales, they determine they can spend a certain amount for new inventory. If they project $25,000 in sales they allow themselves to spend a larger amount on inventory.

Of course, inventory or cost of goods sold, is only one ingredient used in planning cash flow. Businesses need to look at all of their expenses when they make cash flow projections.

A simple eBay business would likely have many of the expenses listed below:

1) eBay fees
2) Auction hosting fees (paid to a service provider like Vendio, Auctiva, or Ink Frog)
3) Shipping and packing supplies
4) Postage (paid to the USPS, Fed Ex, or UPS)
5) Bank fees (PayPal fees, checking accounts, and credit card processing)
6) Gas and mileage for your car
7) Cost of goods (or inventory)
8) Miscellaneous fees (shelving, storage, etc.)
9) Equipment (computers, printers, etc.)

While not an all-inclusive list, this will give you an idea of the expenses you need to track. You also need to track your sources of income.

If you're a typical online seller these are some of the income sources you are likely to encounter:

1) eBay sales
2) Amazon Sales
3) Etsy Sales
4) Shipping income
5) Miscellaneous income

What this book is going to do is help you take a better look at your business income and expenses.

We're going to examine several different methods of tracking your expenses. eBay has a great app – GoDaddy Bookkeeping (formerly known as Outlook) that makes it easy for sellers to record their earnings and expenses. Some sellers prefer simpler methods, such as an Excel spreadsheet or a paper journal.

Accounting solutions such as GoDaddy Bookkeeping can track your sales across multiple platforms, so if you sell on Amazon or Etsy you can automatically import sales information from them. You can set up separate income and sales accounts to make the program more flexible.

In my case, I was able to set up separate income accounts for my paperback, eBook, and audiobook sales so I can track that data alongside of my eBay and Amazon sales. I will go into more detail on this later and show you how to do it.

Before I go any further let me tell you a little more about me, so you can understand why I'm the right guy to help you with your eBay accounting needs.

Table of Contents

Why listen to me

Hey there, Nick Vulich here.

If you're like me, I'm sure you're probably a little skeptical about taking advice from someone without knowing a little bit about them first.

I've been selling on eBay since 1999. Most of my online customers know me as history-bytes, although I've also operated as its old news, back door video, and sports card one.

I've sold 30,004 items for a total of $411,755.44 over the past fifteen years, and that's just on my history-bytes id. Right now I've cut way back on eBay selling to focus on my writing, but I still keep my hat in the game. That way I can stay current with the challenges my readers face every day when they go to sell on eBay.

I've been an eBay Power Seller or Top Rated Seller for most of the past fifteen years, which means I've met eBay's sales and customer satisfaction goals.

Right off, that tells you I'm not coming at you out of left field, with all sorts of half-baked ideas I dreamed up after reading a half-dozen eBay how-to books. Most of the tips I'm going to share with you, I learned from the school of hard-knocks. I learned them from being out there selling every day, experimenting with new products, and new listing methods.

This is the seventh book I've written about selling on eBay. The first two, *Freaking Idiots Guide to Selling on eBay*, and *eBay Unleashed*, are aimed more towards how to get started selling on eBay. *eBay 2014* is directed at more advanced sellers and tackles many of the challenges top rated sellers face in the eBay marketplace. *eBay Subject Matter Expert* suggests a different approach to selling on eBay – building a platform where customers recognize you as an expert in your niche, and buy from you because of your knowledge in that field. *Sell It Online* gives a brief overview of selling on eBay, Amazon, Etsy, and Fiver. *How to Make Money Selling Old Books & Magazines on eBay* talks specifically about what I know best, how to sell books and magazines on eBay.

Taken together these books give you all the information you need to succeed on eBay. My goal is to help you become as successful as you wish to be.

Let's get started…

Getting started

What's that you say? You don't know the difference between a debit and a credit. Balancing your checkbook is a weeklong task. So how are you ever going to figure out business accounting, let alone get the right info together for Uncle Sam?

Don't sweat it.

Modern accounting programs have simplified everything so you don't need to know the difference between a debit and a credit.

If you can punch your sales and expenses into the right category these programs will work their magic and show you the final results – whether you made a profit or a loss.

Get Organized

The first thing you're going to need is a system to organize and store your receipts and records. Some sellers use a file cabinet. Some use expandable file folders. I like to use loose-leaf binders. I get a five inch binder, monthly divider inserts, and storage pocket inserts.

Storing everything this way keeps all of my business records readily accessible, and the binder fits neatly on my bookshelf. I can store fifteen years of business records side-by-side in a relatively small space.

Save your receipts

Get used to it now. You need to save all of your receipts.

When you buy something on line, print out the invoice, punch it with a three hole punch, and store it in your three ring binder under the month of purchase.

Save all of your mortgage or rent receipts, utility bills, phone bills, cable bills, sewer bills, etc. Store them in a zipper pouch in your binder. You're going to need them to file for the home office deduction. It's going to save your thousands of dollars on your taxes every year.

If you purchase supplies at Walmart, Staples, Office Depot, etc. save your receipts in a No. 10 envelope. Label the envelopes by month and store them in a zipper pouch in your binder.

Start writing down your mileage

Go to Walmart, Target, or your office supply superstore and buy a mileage log. They cost about three bucks, and can save you close to a thousand dollars over the course of the year.

Starting today – You need to write down the beginning mileage on your vehicle. Every time you get in the car to run to the post office, pick up supplies, cruise a garage or estate sale, or anything related to your business – write it down. You need to record your beginning and ending mileage. Jot down a quick note about where you went, or why you went there. It doesn't have to be a novel or anything fancy. Post Office, bank, yard sale – just something to leave a trail of how it was business related.

Save all of your auto related receipts as well. The government lets you deduct your actual travel related expenses, or the mileage deduction (56¢ this year), whichever is greater. To ensure the largest deduction you need to save your car payment stubs, insurance payment records, gas receipts, repair bills, oil change receipts, anything related to your car. Grab another No. 10 envelope for each month, and label it auto expenses.

Claim your workspace

In order to claim the home office deduction we talked about earlier you need to devote a portion of your home exclusively to your online business. Pick a room, a portion of a room, your garage, basement, or whatever. Get everything not related to your business out of there, and start setting up your workspace.

Even if you do most of your listing sitting in the recliner in front of the TV you need a separate room for storage, mailing, and quiet time. The space your chair occupies doesn't count as a work area for the home office deduction and neither does the kitchen table if it doubles as a shipping center and a suppertime smorgasbord.

Open a business checking account

You're running a business now. One of the first things you need to do is separate your business and financial expenses.

Open a business checking account, and get a business debit card and credit card. This does two things. In case of an IRS audit, it shows them you are serious about your business. And two, it keeps you from nickel and diming your business to death. The minute you deposit your eBay money in your personal account you're going to start spending it on a Starbucks coffee, a Mickey D's burger, whatever. If you're ever going to accurately track your business earnings and expenses you need to separate it from your personal money.

PayPal is for business

Starting today, you need to make a decision that your PayPal account is a part of your business. Don't make personal purchases with your PayPal account. If you have a PayPal debit card, stop using it to buy pop, gas, groceries, etc. Use it when you pick up shipping supplies, or purchase inventory for your business.

When you do slip up and make a personal purchase with your PayPal account or PayPal debit card make sure you label it as a personal expenditure. That way it won't mess with your accounting records.

Set Money aside for business expansion

Once the money starts pouring into your account it's easy to get caught up in spending it. Decide up front that you're going to reinvest a certain percentage of your profits into expanding your business, whether that means adding new product lines, upgrading your computer system, or updating your work area.

Do this today before the extra money becomes a part of your regular spending habits.

Make a plan, and work your plan

This one ties into setting money aside for business expansion.

After your business has been running for a while it's time to sit down and develop a business plan. Decide where you want to be in six months, a year from now, and five years from now. It doesn't have to be a lengthy document. You can start by jotting down a few notes – I want to double my sales over the next eighteen months, or by this time next year I want to be making $20,000 a year.

As time goes by add to your plan. Make it more specific. Make a list of short term and long term targets, and check them off as you reach them.

In short, make a plan, and work your plan.

Bookkeeping should be an important part of your plan. Business success is measured by numbers.

You don't need to be an accounting genius to be successful selling online, but you do need to know enough to understand your numbers.

In the next section I'm going to give you a list of accounting terms that can come in handy. The more you understand them the better you will be at managing your business.

Here's the very least you need to know about accounting to run your business properly.

Accounting records are recorded in what's called a **general ledger**. It is basically a financial record of a company over a period of time. The information recorded in it is used by accountants and accounting programs to prepare financial statements.

Accountants use what's called a double entry system. A debit on one side is offset by a credit on the other side. The good news is with today's advanced software, business owners don't need to know anything about debits and credits. The program does all of the heavy lifting for you and crunches the numbers.

A **balance sheet** shows a company's assets, liabilities, and owner's equity at a given point in time. The simple formula behind the balance sheet is –

$$assets = liabilities + owner's\ equity$$

A **cash flow statement** shows all of the money a company earns and spends over a period of time. Company's use cash flow projections to help manage their spending, and ensure they have the required money on hand to cover their bills.

A profit and loss statement or **P & L statement** shows whether a business is profitable or not over a period of time. Companies generally prepare P & L statements monthly, quarterly, and yearly.

The general format for the P & L statement is to list income accounts at the top, then expenses, followed by a final line that shows the "bottom line" – or profit and loss.

If you understand these reports you will be more in tune with the financial health of your business.

Accounting terms you need to know

When you talk to your accountant these are some of the terms he is likely to discuss.

All businesses need certain financial reports to help them understand the financial health of their business. The reports you will use the most are the Balance Sheet, General Ledger, Cash Flow Statement, and Profit & Loss Statement.

If you're unsure about how to use these reports, use that as a talking point with your accountant or financial advisor. Probably the most important financial report you need to master is your cash flow statement. It will help you ensure you have the cash available to pay your day-to-day business expenses, and plan for long term growth.

If you understand your Profit & Loss Statement you will better understand where your business is going.

Accounts Receivable. Money your customers owe you for goods or services.

Accounts Payable. Money you owe to your creditors for goods and services purchased from them.

Assets. Property you own, such as inventory, cash, buildings, shipping supplies, etc. Accountants like to break assets down further into current and fixed assets. Current assets are ones that will be used within one year. Fixed assets are ones that a company will hold onto for a longer term such as buildings and automobiles.

Balance sheet. This is a financial report that shows what a company owns and what it owes. The difference represents the owner's equity in the business.

Cash flow. This is the revenue your business is expected to generate over a period of time. Businesses use cash flow projections to plan their future cash needs.

Certified Public Accountant (CPA). A CPA is a certified financial advisor who has met government standards as regards education and experience.

Cost of Goods Sold. The cost of materials used to produce a profit in your business. For an online business the most obvious cost of goods sold is your inventory.

Credit. An accounting entry made on a company's balance sheet. It decreases assets or increases liabilities.

Debit. An accounting entry made on a company's balance sheet. It increases assets or decreases liabilities.

General Ledger. Simply put, this is a record of a company's financial transactions.

Net income. This is the profit a company makes after all expenses are paid. In business terms, it is often called the "bottom line."

Profit and Loss Statement (P & L). The P & L is a financial statement that shows a company's performance during a period of time. Most businesses track their P & L monthly, quarterly, and annually. It helps companies keep tabs on the health of their business by allowing them to review expenses and income. Close study of their P & L helps business catch early trends such as increasing costs or decreasing profits.

GoDaddy Bookkeeping

G oDaddy Bookkeeping is available as an app you can download from eBay's applications bar. Amazon and Etsy sellers can check out the online version by visiting this link http://www.godaddy.com/accounting/accounting-software.aspx?isc=gooob012&ci=87249.

The service was originally known as Outright, and was taken over by GoDaddy last year. It's an online accounting solution that will serve the needs of most users. It automatically imports transaction data from your PayPal account, and posts it to the proper categories. Users can also synch their business credit cards and checking accounts with the service.

For sellers conducting business on multiple platforms GoDaddy Bookkeeping can import transaction data from eBay, Amazon and Etsy. It also works with several invoicing services including FreshBooks, Shoeboxed, and Harvest.

Here's the least you need to know. GoDaddy Bookkeeping is available in the *Applications* tab on your *My eBay* page. Hover your mouse over *Applications* until it shows Manage Applications, click on this and scroll through the list of applications until you come to *Outright*. Click on *Outright*, and select *Try it Free*.

GoDaddy Bookkeeping is available as a monthly ($9.99) or yearly ($99.00) subscription. Choose your poison and follow the prompts to get started.

Overview

The first page you see is your account overview. It contains all of the basic information about your account. In the upper right corner it shows your yearly profit or loss so you can tell at a glance where you stand. Below this is a graph that charts your income and expenses, a pie chart that shows your current month's expenses, and then a list of open invoices.

Below this is a section that shows Invoice Activity. Most online sellers aren't going to use this feature as all of your invoicing is done through eBay, Amazon, Etsy, and your ecommerce storefronts. If you're running a side business where your customers pay through PayPal this is where you would bill your customers for products or services sold.

In the left hand column you'll see four small blue boxes. The first box is labeled *New This Week* and tracks your new sales, and any uncategorized expenses. To view your new transactions or uncategorized expenses click on the number, and it will take you to your general ledger.

The *Money I Have Box* lets you view the balances in your accounts – PayPal, Amazon, and any bank accounts you have connected.

The Money I Owe box shows your liabilities or the money you owe. Some of the accounts shown here are your eBay balance, and money owed to Amazon and Etsy for seller fees.

The last box is labeled *Taxes*. It shows you several key tax indicators for your business. The first line shows your estimated quarterly tax payment, and when it is due. The mileage line shows your year to date mileage expenses. When you click on mileage it takes you to your general ledger and lets you log your mileage. The last line shows your *Sales Tax Liability*, so you always know how much you owe.

Below the four blue boxes you should see two blue bars. *Add Account* lets you add your various seller accounts, PayPal Account, and any bank accounts you want to tie into GoDaddy Bookkeeping. *Refresh All* imports data from your connected accounts so that you're viewing the most recent information available.

If you scroll back up to the top of the page you'll see your six control tabs – Overview, Income, Expenses, Reports, Taxes, and Manage. When you click on any of these they open more program options.

Before I describe the control tabs there's one other item I should cover. Sometimes a tan bar will be displayed just below the control tab. It shows program alerts or problems GoDaddy Bookkeeping may be experiencing with your account. When you click on the Fix It highlight it will walk you through solving the problem so you can get your program up and running correctly again.

———————————

You can view your profit & loss statement anytime by clicking on the *view details* tab underneath where it says *(Year) Profit & Loss* on the GoDaddy Bookkeeping *Overview* page.

Your Profit & Loss statement gives you a quick overview of the financial health of your business. The top section shows your sources of income, and the bottom section details your expenses. The final line shows your "bottom line," or the actual profit or loss your business is making.

The default view for your P & L is the previous twelve months, but you have the option to change that any time you'd like. Scroll up to the top of the page under *Profit & Loss* where you see *ending*. You can choose the ending month or year, or you can change the time period to day, week, month, quarter, or year. To return to the chart select the chart icon on the right hand side.

If you want to take a closer look at a transaction all of the items on your P & L are clickable. Select the one you want to examine and it will take you to the general ledger page for that category.

Moving back down to the bottom of the page you will see two tabs at the far right side. Export lets you transfer P & L information to a Microsoft Excel file. Selecting print will give you a hard copy of your P & L.

Income

The income tab lets you manage your online income accounts. When you click on income it takes you to your general ledger page for income, and you can view your most recent transactions.

Once again, all of the transactions displayed are clickable. If you want to edit a transaction select it, and make the needed corrections.

What I recommend here is to set up categories for all of your income transactions so you can track where your money is coming from. When GoDaddy Bookkeeping imports income transactions it brings all of them in under the general "sales" heading. If you're just selling on one venue, such as eBay or Amazon, that's not a problem. If you sell across multiple platforms it's important to know the source your money is coming from. This way you can take corrective action if a sales venue is underperforming.

The first thing you need to know is every time you make a sale GoDaddy Bookkeeping records it as two separate transactions. The merchandise portion is recorded under the heading "sales." If you charged postage on the transaction it is logged as "shipping income."

If you want to add additional sales categories select a transaction, and then scroll down the page until you see a heading labeled *Good to Know*. Over to the right hand side you will see a link labeled *Manage Categories*. Select it. This shows you a chart of your current income categories. To add a category select *New income Category*. Categorize it as *Business* or *Nonbusiness*, and then name the new category. After doing this you need to select a tax category. To tie the category you created to sales you would choose *gross receipts or sales*. Select *create*, and your new category is ready to use.

To give you an idea about how to use this, I added the following categories to my income account – eBay sales, Amazon, Bonanza, *eBid*, bidStart, Kindle, Create Space, and

Audible. By doing this I can keep separate tabs on each of my sales channels. It gives me better control over my business, and allows me to spot patterns early as they're beginning to emerge.

After you set up your income categories you need to assign each individual transaction to the proper category. The easiest way to do this is from the Overview page. Select *view details* to see your P & L. Click on *sales* in the income section of your P & L. This will pull up all of your unassigned items. Select each item separately, and assign it to the proper income account. This step is pretty straightforward and should take just a few moments a day.

Whenever you're working on your P & L you also want to take a look at your uncategorized expenses. They're listed at the bottom of the P & L, just before you see your bottom line. Most items are categorized when they're imported, but there are usually a few uncategorized items, either because you purchased from a new supplier and GoDaddy Bookkeeping doesn't know how to classify it, or because the items you purchased from that supplier may fit into several different expense categories. Click on the individual unclassified transactions and assign them to the proper category.

If you do this every time you open your program it will only take a few minutes of your time, and it will ensure your P & L is up-to-date and accurate.

Expenses

When you select expenses it brings up the general ledger view for your business expenses.

Similar to the income category you can set up personalized categories to customize GoDaddy Bookkeeping for your business needs. Select an individual expense to enter the edit mode. Scroll down the page until you see the heading *Good to Know*. Move your mouse to the far right of the page and click on *manage categories*. Select *new expense category* and follow the prompts. Categorize the expense as a business or nonbusiness expense and name it. Scroll through the *tax category list* to tie your new expense to the proper category, and then select *Create*.

I would suggest setting up custom categories for your internet and cell phone providers, storage space rental, etc.

I find it useful to lump a few expense categories together. The main category I do this with is postage. I throw all of my shipping expenses in there – boxes, packing tape, stay free mailers, peanuts, you name it. The reason I do this is it makes it easier to compare my shipping expenses and shipping income. As long as the shipping income is equal to or more than my shipping expense, I know I'm on the right track. When they get out of whack it's time for an intervention to determine what went wrong.

With my other expenses my main concern is that they're consistent from month-to-month. If one month is way up without a similar bump in sales it's time to investigate what happened. Sometime it's a special purchase I had the opportunity to make; sometimes a number was entered wrong. The key thing is to watch your numbers and react quickly when you see that something is out of whack.

Reports

When you select reports it brings you to your Profit and loss statement. GoDaddy bookkeeping always shows you the chart first. Select *view as table* to see your P & L Statement.

If you're running a business you should know these numbers forwards and backwards. Growth is good, but I like to see consistent numbers across the board.

When I'm comparing my book sales numbers, the first thing I do is compare them with the last few months. If sales seem unusually low I take a peek at last year's numbers to see if it's a seasonal trend. You should do the same thing.

Online sales are always slower in summer. They normally pick up by late August and run strong through spring. February is a little iffy – it can go either way. The first half of November can be the same way waiting for Christmas buying to kick in.

Key point: Use your P & L to help forecast fluctuations in your business. Study it for trends, where sales are increasing or decreasing, or where expenses are rising. Put on your detective hat and figure out what's happening. Doing this will make you a better business person, and help your business to grow stronger over the long haul.

Taxes

The taxes section helps you with three specific areas.

1) It provides your Schedule C information to make tax time a breeze. Just transfer over the numbers and you're ready to file. Keep in mind you're still going to need a tax advisor or a good tax program like TurboTax Business or HR Block Business. GoDaddy Bookkeeping doesn't figure the home office deduction, tax credits, etc. They just provide you with the raw numbers to fill out your Schedule C.

2) GoDaddy tracks your sales taxes due, so it's easy to file and submit your state reports. As long as you have eBay, Amazon, and Etsy set up to collect sales tax in your state, GoDaddy Bookkeeping will track all of the information for you.

3) Every time you log into your account you are able to see your estimated tax payments and the date they are due. This way the due date and the amount you owe won't sneak up on you.

Manage

When you select manage it displays a list of all the accounts you have connected to GoDaddy Bookkeeping. If any of the accounts have errors you will see a tan bar displayed by them. Click on the blue *Fix It* link to take care of account issues.

If you want to connect more accounts, select *Add an Account* at the top of the page

———————————

Good to know

You can easily reassign categories if something appears is mis-categorized.

Most often when this happens it's because the program does not recognize how to classify the transaction. To fix the problem select the item that needs to be classified. At the far right it will say uncategorized item, select the correct category from the drop down box, and press save.

You will also need to re-categorize items when you make a non-business related purchase. GoDaddy Bookkeeping has a *personal expense* category you can assign the item to so it is removed from your business records. If you sell a personal item and receive payment for an item through your PayPal account you can reassign it to the *personal income* category.

Best advice

Keep a close eye on your accounting program. Update it every few days. It's easier to catch errors when just a few items are displayed. If you let it go too long, a large list of items to re-categorize can seem overwhelming.

Using an Excel spreadsheet

What if you want to keep track of your income and expenses the old fashioned way – using an Excel spreadsheet or a hand written ledger?

No problem.

If you use Excel you need to set up your income and expense categories similar to the way accounting programs do. It should look something like this –

Income

- eBay sales

- Amazon sales

- Etsy sales

- Bonanza sales

- bidStart sales

- Sales tax collected

- Shipping income

Expenses

- Cost of goods sold

- eBay fees

- Amazon fees

- Etsy fees

- Bonanza fees

- Internet expenses

- Phone

- Utilities

- Rent

- Computer equipment

- Software

- Professional fees

- Postage

- Mailing supplies

- Office supplies

Bottom Line

The easiest way to track your expenses is in a simple ledger style. Run your categories down the right hand side of the page. Put your days across the top of the page. Leave room to subtotal your income and expenses. At the very bottom you should have a space for your "bottom line" or profit and loss.

Assign a separate page for each month. At the end of each month transfer all of the information over to a page with yearly totals. Excel users have an advantage here because you can set these items to automatically update.

What I've outlined here is a very simple system, but it will give you all the information you need to manage your business. By looking over your income and expenses you should be able to spot trends and identify cash flow problems.

The best advice I can give you is to try to update your information every day or two. If you leave it go until the end of the month the task is going to seem overwhelming.

What about QuickBooks

QuickBooks used to be my accounting program of choice. Late last year they retired the QuickBooks Connector which automatically imported sales and expense data from eBay and PayPal. Since then it has lost most of its appeal as an accounting system for online sellers.

Yes. You can still import data automatically, but now you need to locate a third party provider, and pay them extra to do the work for you. QuickBooks recommended provider is ecc cloud. You can check them out by following this link http://www.webgility.com/ecc-cloud/quickbooks-online-integration-ecommerce.php.

Ecc cloud charges from $15.00 to $149.00 per month for their services based upon the number of transactions you need to import.

You can read more of QuickBooks spiel about QuickBooks for eBay Business Owners by checking out this link http://quickbooks.intuit.com/ebay-business/.

Obviously, I don't think QuickBooks is a good solution for most sellers, so why'd I bring it up here?

QuickBooks is a full featured accounting program that helps you run a business of any size. If you're running a brick and mortar location, an online business, managing a large inventory, and invoicing customers you need a program like

QuickBooks to tie it all together. In this case, paying the extra fees to a 3rd party service provider may be well worth it.

For everyday online sellers making fewer than five hundred monthly transactions GoDaddy Bookkeeping is going to handle all of your accounting needs. It's less expensive, has a short learning curve, and is easy to use.

My advice is to stick with GoDaddy Bookkeeping until you outgrow it, or have a bunch of extra cash jingling around in your pockets that you just have to spend.

Working with an accountant

I t takes some of us longer to acknowledge we need help than it does others.

I interviewed my first accountant about two years after I started selling online. I was making about $1,500 a month selling on eBay at that time and I was starting to get it all together. I had a business checking account, a business credit card, and had just upgraded all of my computer equipment.

Things were looking good, and I decided having an accountant on my side could be the ace-in-the-hole I needed to be more successful.

Ok. I made my appointment. Gathered up all my receipts, and printed out my reports from QuickBooks. In effect, I was ready to do battle.

I walked in, placed my bundles on the desk, and sat down opposite the accountant. I was promised a free hour's consultation, and I made sure to get in as many questions as I could. I suppose I wanted to get my money's worth – even if it was a free appointment.

When I walked out of that office I was psyched up and sure he was the guy. And, yet – I didn't add an accountant to my team for another five years. Why? Because I couldn't justify the $65.00 an hour fee several times a year.

It doesn't make any sense now. But sixty-five bucks is sixty-five bucks, and thirteen years ago, that was a lot of money.

Let me tell you what I've learned over the last ten years that justifies every penny I pay my accountant.

Perhaps the biggest reason is peace-of-mind. I'm a seat-of-the-pants type of guy, which means I normally just jump into things and do them the best I can. While that sometimes works selling on eBay or writing books, it doesn't always work the best when you're trying to manage your finances.

I still do my day-to-day accounting and my taxes myself, but I'm smart enough now to have someone peek over my shoulder now and then to make sure I'm on the right track. Sometimes I make stupid mistakes, overlook important details, or just can't see obvious mistakes. An extra set of eyes on my paperwork can point out these hidden boners (sorry for that word, but it is appropriate here).

Fortunately most of my mistakes have been small ones that are easily fixable. But, the peace-of-mind thing is still an important factor that keeps me paying my accountant's bill.

It's an extra eye on my paperwork pointing out that I spent too much on inventory last quarter, or I probably don't need to buy a new laptop every year, or have the fanciest iPhone each time they come out. Sometimes you don't see (or don't want to see) your own crazy spending habits.

Let's talk about you for a minute.

What can working with an accountant do for your business? Obviously, there's that peace-of-mind thing. They can also –

1) Help you determine how much you should pay for your quarterly tax payments.

2) Find extra deductions and credits to reduce your taxes and help you receive larger refunds.

3) Help you understand the breakeven point for your business so that you know how many sales you need to make just to cover your bills.

4) By challenging your spending habits, they can help you increase profits and make better purchasing decisions.

5) If your business is seasonal, depending more upon Christmas or summertime sales, an accountant can help you smooth out cash flow fluctuations so you can keep your business running smoothly year around.

6) Set up a retirement plan that allows you to maximize current earnings while saving more money for retirement.

7) A good accountant can help you plan for growth, or to reach other stretch goals you may have for your business.

With all of that said, how do you find a good accountant that you can work with?

Most accountants offer a free consultation. This is a chance for you to meet with them and kick the tires a little. Normally the accountant will tell you a little bit about how they like to do business and what they can do for you, and then they will throw the ball into your court and let you ask some questions.

My suggestion is to make up a list of questions before your appointment.

Ask questions about costs. Ask about how often you need to consult with them? Ask what the accountant expects from you? What papers do they need you to supply? If you're looking for help incorporating your business or setting up a retirement plan, nail down the costs. If you're looking for tips to help grow your business, make sure they have experience dealing with businesses similar to your own. Get references, and be sure to check them out.

Most importantly, don't rush into any arrangement. Interview at least two or three accountants until you find someone you feel comfortable working with.

One final note: Depending upon the accountant you chose to work with you may be asked to provide an "accountant's copy" each time you come in. This makes it easier for your accountant to keep tabs on your business, and check for errors in your record keeping.

If your accountant requires an "accountant's copy" to work with you're going to need to switch to QuickBooks. GoDaddy Bookkeeping does not offer this feature.

The lowdown on taxes

Remember that old saying, "The only thing certain in life is death and taxes." Running a business is all about collecting and paying taxes.

Here are just a few of the different taxes you're going to be dealing with in your eBay business.

1) Sales & use taxes
2) Estimated taxes
3) Self-employment taxes
4) Unemployment tax
5) State and Federal Income Taxes

We're going to talk a little bit about each of these taxes – What they are? How they affect your business? And, what you need to do to stay on the right side of the IRS and your local tax authorities.

1) **Sales & use taxes**. Forty-five states require residents to pay a sales tax when they purchase property within that state. If you are an online seller and make a sale within your home state, you are required by law to collect the proper sales tax on it, and remit the payment to your state tax authority. Failure to collect sales tax could put you on the wrong side of tax authorities if your sales are audited.

To collect taxes you need to apply for a sales and use tax permit (sometimes called a resale permit) from your state. There is normally no charge for it, but some states may require you to make a deposit based upon the volume of transactions you are expected to handle. You will be asked a few quick questions about your business, your sales channel, and your expected sales revenue. Once you receive your permit you are required to collect tax on every transaction you process in your home state. Most states base your payment period upon your expected tax collections. As a result you may have to remit payments monthly, quarterly, or annually.

Use tax is one of the most overlooked or misunderstood taxes. The way it's supposed to work is if you purchase something from outside of your home state and don't pay sales tax, you're supposed to fess up on your state income tax form and pay the appropriate tax. As you can probably guess, that rarely happens.

A good example of an item that would qualify for use tax is if you purchase your mailers from an out of state supplier on eBay. They ship them to you without charging sales tax. Because no sales tax was charged on this transaction when you purchased it, you are obligated to pay a use tax to make up for it.

The same thing is true for non-business owners. If you order clothes from a seller on eBay or Amazon and aren't charged sales tax you are obligated to declare the transaction on your state income tax return, and pay the appropriate sales tax on it.

If you intend to purchase items from a wholesaler they will require you to provide them with a state tax id. If you can't produce a tax id, some wholesalers will refuse to do business with you, others will insist on charging you sales tax on all of your purchases. You can also use your tax permit to eliminate sales taxes when you are purchasing items for resale from other retailers. So the next time you scoop up a cartload of closeouts at the outlet mall you can save yourself a bundle by not having to pay the sales tax.

2) **Estimated taxes**. If you are self-employed you are required to pay estimated taxes to the IRS and to your state tax authority. Quarterly taxes are due April 15, July 15, October 15, and January 15. Tax programs such as TurboTax and H R Block will help you estimate your quarterly taxes. If you use GoDaddy Bookkeeping it will show you your estimated taxes due. GoDaddy also shows your sales tax liability.

Keep in mind most of these programs estimate your taxes based on last year's income, or in the case of GoDaddy Bookkeeping they base their estimates on your trending income. If your income is sporadic or changes from year to year you may want to consult with an accountant or tax advisor to ensure you're paying in the proper amount.

If you pay in less than a certain percentage of the amount that is due you may wind up having to pay extra fees and penalties.

3) **Self-employment taxes** are similar to Social Security and Medicare taxes charged to people who work for an employer. The only difference is self-employed persons need to self-report

these taxes, and pay both the employer's and the employee's share.

Self-employment taxes are figured on Schedule SE of your IRS Form 1040. In 2014 the self-employment tax rate was 15.3% - 12.4% for Social Security, and 2.9% for Medicare. In 2014 the amount of income subject to the portion for Social Security tax was capped at $117,000. There is no cap for the Medicare tax portion of self-employment tax.

You can deduct the employer portion of your self-employment tax (approximately 50 percent) when you figure your adjusted gross income for Federal taxes.

4) **Unemployment taxes**. If you hire employees to work in your online business you are required to pay unemployment taxes. These vary by state. Just keep in mind, there is a separate state and Federal tax due.

See Publication 926 for more information and a list of state taxing authorities.
http://www.irs.gov/publications/p926/index.html

5) **Federal and state taxes**. When most online sellers think about taxes, these are what come to mind.

Some online sellers try to avoid paying income taxes on their earnings, or think they're just for big time sellers. The truth is if you make as little as one dollar selling online you are required to report it for income tax purposes.

To keep everyone honest, the government imposed mandatory reporting requirements upon PayPal. If more than $20,000 is deposited into your PayPal account during the course of the year, PayPal is required to report it to the IRS on form 1099-K.

To view your form 1099-K sign into your PayPal Account, hover your pointer over the **history** tab, and this will bring up a drop down menu. You want to click on **tax documents**, and this will give you the option to view a PDF file of your 1099-K, if one was generated for you.

At this time you are not required to submit the PayPal 1099-K with your income tax filing, but you should be sure you are reporting at least as much income as is shown on it. You can be sure the IRS is matching them up, and taking a close look at your 1099-K, and the income you report on your tax return.

_____

That's the very least you need to know about taxes and you're online business. Here are a few more tips that can help you out when the time comes to prepare your Federal and state tax forms.

Business income is reported on Schedule C of your Form 1040.

Several tax programs are available to make filing your business taxes easier. The two I've had the most experience working with are TurboTax Business and H R Block Premium or H R Block Premium & Business. Each of these programs will conduct a fact finding interview with you about your business, and walk you step-by-step through filing your tax return.

If you pay extra for the premium version of GoDaddy Bookkeeping it will generate a paper version of your Schedule C with all of the information you need to key into your 1040 Tax Form. One other quick tip. If you don't pay for the premium version of GoDaddy Bookkeeping all of your information previous to the current twelve month will be hidden from your view. To ensure you don't lose any important financial data print a copy of your P & L, and your monthly statements before the end of January. If you don't, you will need to subscribe to the premium version to recover your information.

Even if you use an accountant or tax preparer doing your taxes first can save you hundreds of dollars when it comes time to file your taxes. This way all of the information is gathered together and entered in the correct areas on your tax return. All your tax professional needs to do is review everything to make sure there was nothing you overlooked or left out.

Most common tax deductions

One of the perks of being a business owner is the ability to shift some of your income by taking advantage of various business deductions. Here are some of the most common business deductions taken by online business owners.

Home Office Deduction. Many business owners are afraid to claim the home office deduction because they've heard the IRS targets filers who take it. That's pretty much one of those urban legends that gets bigger every time it's told.

The home office deduction is every online seller's best friend, and can save you thousands of dollars on your taxes if you use it properly.

Here are the IRS rules for taking the home office deduction:

1) Your home must be your principal place of business.
2) You must use the area of your home (a room, or portion of a room) exclusively to conduct business. This means if you do all of your work at your kitchen table, you would not qualify for the home office deduction, because you don't use that area exclusively for business. If, on the other hand, you devote an extra bedroom, basement, or garage exclusively to conducting the activities of your online business then this space would qualify for the home office deduction.

To learn more about the home office deduction you can check out Publication 587. http://www.irs.gov/publications/p587/index.html

The methods for calculating the home office deduction changed in 2013, so even if you have taken it in the past you may want to brush up on the new guidelines.

Mileage Deduction. If you use your vehicle while conducting your business you are able to deduct your expenses. Business owners can take either the standard mileage deduction, or deduct the actual expenses incurred for the use of the vehicle in their business.

To take the mileage deduction you need to record all of the miles your car is driven for personal and for business use. I would recommend purchasing a mileage log. You can find one in the office supply section at Walmart or Target, or at larger office supply stores such as Office Max, Staples, or Office Depot. They run about $3.00, and are small enough to slip under your visor or into your glove box.

Each time you head to the post office, run to the store for mailing supplies, or to a yard sale or estate sale to pick up new inventory make sure to record your beginning and ending mileage.

In 2014 the standard mileage deduction was 56¢ per business mile driven. If you opt to deduct actual expenses, make sure to record all of your expenses for car payments, insurance, repairs, tires, oil changes, and gasoline. You can then deduct the percentage of expenses based on the miles driven for business usage.

Travel. Did you ever want to visit California or Hawaii, but weren't sure you could afford it?. The cost of travel is fully deductible as long as it is business related.

Let's say you're ready for a vacation and eBay is having one of its events in Scottsdale. You are able to deduct all of your expenses – airfare, car rentals, cabs, motels, food, and admission – as long as they are related to the event. If your spouse helps out in your business, their expenses would be covered as well. If you decide to make a real vacation of it and bring the kids along too, you would not be able to deduct expenses for their travel, food, lodging, etc. because they do not participate in the business.

The travel expense deduction can also be used to cover day trips out of town. If you visit an estate sale or auction several hundred miles away all of your expenses related to the buying trip would be deductible. Again, if you bring along the kids or someone unrelated to your business, their expenses would not be covered.

Computers, printers, office supplies. Are you a techie? Have you always wanted to own the latest, greatest gadgets, but wished you had a rich uncle to help you out with the payments?

Uncle Sam can come to the rescue here too. You can deduct the price of a new computer, printer, cell phone, iPad, or any other gadget that you regularly use in your online business. The only hitch is the item needs to be for your business use only.

You have the option of depreciating the expense of your purchase over the expected life of the item, or in most cases, you can deduct the full value of the item in the year it is purchased.

Internet, cell phone, etc. If you purchase a separate cell phone or internet service for your business you can deduct the full cost of them as a business expense. If you use them for business and personal use, you can only deduct the portion of the service you use for business.

If you're on track to make a little too much money this year and are worried about paying extra taxes, look at some of these ideas as ways to shift your tax burden. Once again, don't go crazy. Before you rush off on that junket to Hawaii or Europe, consult with your tax advisor first, to make sure the trip is deductible in your situation.

———————————

Two other ideas while we're on the subject of tax deductions. You can use your business income to help fund your retirement, or to shift money to your kids by employing them to work in your business.

When you own your own business, you are allowed to fund a personal retirement account, 401K, SEP IRA, or KEOGH. The individual details are beyond the scope of this book; consult a tax professional for more details.

If you have kids, put them to work for your company and pay them the money you would have given them anyway. If you have college age kids, this is a good way of helping them pay their way through college while deducting the expense from your business. Keep in mind when you do this it is just like hiring a regular employee. You need to pay unemployment taxes, and provide a W-2 at the end of the year.

Business permits, licenses, & such

Most eBay sellers run their businesses out of their homes. The majority of their neighbors don't know anything about it, except for the frequent comings and goings of the mail trucks, UPS vans, and Fed Ex guys.

As such, most eBay sellers don't bother with licenses or permits. They go about their daily routine pretty much unaware they may be breaking local codes and regulations.

What I'm going to do here is talk a little bit about the different licenses and permits a typical eBay business owner might bump up against, and give you a few tips on how to get them.

DBA (Doing Business As). If you conduct your business using an assumed (fictitious) name you are required to record your information with the city clerk's office or county clerk's office depending upon where you live. Sometimes you can fill out the form online. Other times you will be required to go into the appropriate office, and pay a small fee. They check to see if the name is being used by another company in your area. If it is you will need to pick a new name. Banks will require a copy of your DBA if you attempt to open an account in your business's name.

Business License. Most cities and counties require a license to conduct business within their boundaries. The fees vary based upon the type of business you run. Where I live you apply for a license with the city's department of revenue. If you are unsure where to apply for a business license in your area Google "city name business license."

EIN (Employer identification Number). Most online businesses conduct their business using the owner's social security number. If you prefer not to share that information you can apply to the IRS for an EIN. Here is a link to apply for an EIN online https://www.us-tax-id-number.com/?gclid=CJaB3Kq_jr4CFckWMgod63cAbQ.

Home Business Permit. Some municipalities require homeowners to register if they are conducting a business out of their home. Call your city clerk's office to learn more about your areas licensing requirements.

Sales & Use Tax Permit. If you will be making sales to residents within the boundaries of your state you will be required to collect sales tax. Contact your state department of revenue for more information.

The SBA offers an excellent website covering local business licenses that may be required. They even have a search feature where you can enter your zip code, and it will return a list of business licenses and permits you may require. Follow this link for more details http://www.sba.gov/licenses-and-permits

Choosing your business status

How you structure your business is an important factor in how much money you will keep at the end of the year.

Most eBay businesses will take one of the following structures.

1) Sole proprietorship
2) Partnership
3) Corporation
4) Small business corporation (Subchapter S)

Sole proprietorship

A sole proprietorship is the simplest form of business entity. It is run by one person with no distinction between the individual and the business. If the business makes money you keep all of the profits. If the business loses money, you are responsible for all of the losses.

Most sole proprietorships are conducted using the business owner's name. If you choose to run it under a different name you may need to file a DBA (Doing Business As). Normally you would need to register your business with the City Clerk's Office or a county office and pay a small fee. They will check to see if the name you want to use is already in use. If it is being used by another business you will need to choose another name.

Your business income should be recorded on Schedule C of your IRS 1040 tax form, and is taxed at your normal rate.

The major disadvantage of a sole proprietorship is you are 100% responsible for business liabilities. If you sell defective products or someone gets hurt on your business premises you are fully responsible and can be sued for liability.

Partnership

A partnership is a business relationship between two or more people. Partners normally sign a partnership agreement. Each of them contributes a certain amount of capital and labor, and shares in the profits or losses of the business.

Partners can share equally in the profits, or certain partners may have a larger percentage of ownership based upon the partnership agreement. Income is reported to each partner on a form called a Schedule K-1.

The disadvantage again is partners are fully responsible for any liabilities contracted by the business.

Corporation

A corporation is an independent legal entity owned by its shareholders. The business is registered with the State Corporation Department or Secretary of State's Office. They are required to have business licenses and permits, and to file quarterly and annual reports with the state they are incorporated in.

Corporations are normally owned by a large number of people who are issued shares in exchange for investing capital in the business.

Shareholders in the corporation receive income in the form of dividends. The biggest advantage of a corporation is income is taxed at a lower corporate rate, and liability is limited to the money you have invested in the corporation.

Subchapter S Corporation

Subchapter S corporations pass earnings and losses through to shareholders for federal tax purposes. Shareholders report income on their personal tax returns and pay taxes at their normal rate.

To qualify as an S Corporation the corporation must file Form 2553 Election by a Small Business Corporation. http://www.irs.gov/pub/irs-pdf/f2553.pdf

S Corporations have many advantages that make them attractive to online business owners.

1) Your assets are protected. The most you can lose as an investor is the money you have invested in the corporation.

2) Ability to reduce self-employment tax liability by paying yourself a portion of income as salary and as dividends.

3) Pass through taxation which allows owners to report losses or earnings on their personal tax returns.

4) It opens up new possibilities in offering yourself corporate perks such as better retirement plans, writing off college expenses, and other benefits. Be sure to consult with a qualified tax advisor before implementing any of these ideas.

Odds are most online businesses will begin life as a sole proprietorship and scale up as the business grows.

Wrapping it all up

In the end your success isn't determined by how much money you take in, it's determined by how much money you keep after covering your expenses and paying the taxman. If you want to make a profit you need to take in more money than you spend.

Keep in mind I'm not a lawyer or an accountant. The information I've given you is what has worked best for myself, and other sellers I have worked with. Before you make any business decisions you should consult with a lawyer or an accountant to determine how it will affect your individual situation.

With that said, take some time to implement your accounting solutions. Don't jump into them head first without giving them a little thought first.

If you're on the line trying to decide whether to use GoDaddy Bookkeeping, a spreadsheet, or a handwritten journal my suggestion would be to use GoDaddy Bookkeeping. Because it is automated it will help ensure you record all of your sales and expenses.

In my case, I normally make all of my business related purchases with either PayPal or my PayPal Debit card. As a result they all show up in my accounting stream. On those rare occasions I make a personal purchase from those sources I can mark it as a personal expense and back it out of the program. My other purchases are automatically assigned to the proper category, or for those purchases I make that qualify for a number of categories, I can manually assign them to the proper account.

Final takeaway, I rarely miss recording an expense, and I never miss recording a sale. As a result I can be 99.99% sure all my accounting information is accurate and up-to-date for the IRS.

You can't ask for better than that.

Good luck! and great selling everyone.

Further reading

Accounting for Dummies by John A. Tracy

Bookkeeping for Dummies by Lita Epstein

Incorporate Your Business: A Legal Guide to Forming a Corporation in Your State by Anthony Mancuso

J. K. Lasser's From eBay to Mary Kay: Taxes Made Easy for Your Home Business by Gary W. Carter

QuickBooks 2013 & Accounting for Dummies eBook Set by Stephen L. Nelson and John A. Tracy

Tax Loopholes for eBay Sellers: Pay Less Tax and Make More Money by Diane Kennedy and Janice Elms

The Complete Tax Guide for E-Commerce Retailers Including Amazon & eBay Sellers: How Online Sellers Can Stay in Compliance with the IRS & State Tax Laws by Martha Maeda

The eBay Sellers Tax & Legal Answer Book: Everything You Need to Know to Keep the Government Off Your Back by Ennico Cliff

Before you go

The hank you for reading this book. If you enjoyed it, or found it helpful, I'd be grateful if you'd post a short review. Your review really does help. It helps other readers decide if this book would be a good investment for them, and it helps me to make this an even better book for you. I personally read all of the reviews my books receive, and based on what readers tell me, I can make my books even better, and include the kind of information readers want and need.

Thanks again for choosing my book, and here's wishing you great success in your online selling.

Amazon page: amazon.com/author/nickvulich

Blog: http://www.indieauthorstoolbox.com/

Email: hi@nickvulich.com

Bonus excerpt

(This is an excerpt from my most recent book – **Indie Author's Toolbox.** *If you've ever wanted to self-publish your own book,* Indie Author's Toolbox *is the ultimate reference. You will learn how to select a hot subject, how to optimize your book on and off of Amazon, and how to market your book so you can get the power of Amazon behind you – helping to promote your book.)*

Optimize your book on Amazon

Psst! Do you wanna know a secret?

There are no secrets. No tricks. No magical incantations you can invoke to sell more books on Amazon, or any other online book site for that matter.

Selling more books is all about how you manage the basics.

It's about -

1) Writing a good book

2) Selecting a killer title

3) Creating an attention grabbing cover

4) Writing a book description that compels readers to click the buy button

5) Choosing keywords that drive searchers to your book

6) Ensuring your "look inside" sample sells your book

If you can do these six steps well your book is going to sell. Misfire on any of them, and you're going to have problems.

Just so you know some of the advice I'm going to give you here goes contrary to what you're going to get from most of the "experts." In my two years of indie publishing, I've taken a lot of wrong turns. I've been fed a lot of bad advice. All I can tell you is what has worked best for me. Best advice I can give you is to experiment often. Don't be afraid to try new things. Keep the ones that work, discard the ones that don't. Keep building your bag of tricks, and over time you'll develop a system that'll work for you.

With that said, let's dig deeper into each step and see how you can use them to position your book for success.

Write a good book. Abraham Lincoln said it best, "You can fool all the people some of the time, and some of the people all the time, but you cannot fool all the people all the time."

If you don't have a good book, the reviews are going to catch up to you, and people are going to stop buying your book. Sure. You can sell a few copies of a bad book. Sometimes you can sell a whole lot of copies, but eventually the reviews are going to kill your career.

There are a lot of Kindle advice writers telling aspiring authors you don't have to write well. Don't waste too much time editing your work. Just do the best you can, and get your book out there. Sell a few copies, and then write your next book.

Last year, or the year before, that advice might have worked. But readers are getting smarter. They've downloaded a lot of worthless crap over the past few years, and they're tired of it. If you don't believe me, read the reviews. Most readers are honest, and they call it like they see it. If you're book smells like a load of horse hockey, they're going to say it. If enough readers jump on the band wagon, there's no going back.

Forget the books that tell you how to write a book before breakfast, over your lunch break, or on a roll of toilet paper while you're sitting on the throne. At the same time, forget the books that tell you you can write a book in seven days, twenty-one days, or even thirty days. The fact is you can write a book in the time it takes you, no sooner, and no later.

There appears to be a fundamental disconnect between what readers want, and what some writers think readers want. Many writers believe readers want to read short books. The majority of reviewers say just the opposite – here are a few of the reviews major novelists recently received for their Kindle Shorts.

. *A throw away sixty pages.* **Lee Child**

. *Don't waste time and money buying the ads, wait for the book itself.* **Janet Evanovich**

. *It's so short it isn't even a short story.* **Dean Koontz**.

. *Good writing for the beginning of a novel, with no real ending.* **Steven King**

No matter what anyone tells you, most readers don't like short. It makes them feel like they missed out on something, or that the writer was just out to take their money. Consider this the next time you go to publish a short manuscript.

The key to selling more books is to write a complete book that leaves readers satisfied. If you can do this, you're golden. You will get enthusiastic reviews. Readers will tell their friends about you. They will race out to buy your books the first day they're released.

Select a killer title. Too many writers try to stuff a load of keywords into their title hoping they can game the system. Search engines may find keyword bloated titles enticing, but real readers are turned off by titles too big to fit on the book cover. They can't remember them. They don't understand them. They don't know what to think about books that use them.

Short is better.

One to three words is the perfect length for a title. It's easy to remember. There's very little chance for confusion. As a result, you're going to sell more books.

Check out the following five titles. They're short. They're memorable. They do a good job of revealing what the book is about. And, if I didn't mention it, they're selling a lot of books.

. *Story $elling* by Nick Nanton & J. W. Dicks

. *eBay Seller Secrets* by Ann Eckhart

. *Declutter your Inbox* by S. J. Scott

. *Killing Jesus* by Bill O'Reilly

. *Email Marketing* Blueprint by Steve Scott

Compare that to these titles.

. *7 Steps to Sales Scripts for B2B Appointment Setting* by Scott Channell

. *How I Make Money Every Day Automatically When Others Sell on eBay* by Xavier Zimms

. *Author's Quick Guide to Making Money with your 99¢ Kindle Books* by Kristen Eckstein

. *How to Write and Publish your Book on Amazon and on Kindle* by Eldes Saullo

. *How to Write a Kindle Book that People Want to Buy before Breakfast* by James Bedford

Use your main keyword in your title. Use a combination of two or three keywords. Don't string together a series of two or three keyword phrases in your title. It doesn't make sense.

Instead, write a short title. Follow it up with an awesome subtitle that tells readers a little more about the subject matter of your book. Once again, keep the subtitle short. Less than ten words are best. Include your most relevant keywords in your title and subtitle. Place your other search terms where they belong – in your book tags, and in your description.

Make your cover sizzle. Readers are going to be attracted to your book by three things – the title, the cover, and the buzz surrounding it.

Whatever you do, don't design your cover yourself. No matter how good you think you are, or how great you think your idea is, don't design your own cover. Don't let your best friend, or baby sister do it either. Your cover is too important to be left to chance.

I gotta admit I'm a serial Fiverr. I've outsourced 179 graphic design gigs on Fiverr in the last six months. Some of the work you receive is so-so, but a lot of the gigs posted on Fiverr deliver professional quality designs. The results, like anything else, depend upon the effort you put into it.

I use **rroxx** for most of my covers. He does great work, and my projects are always delivered on time. Here's the link to his gig if you want to check it out http://www.fiverr.com/rroxx/create-awesome-professional-ebook-cover-design.

You can also outsource your cover on Elance, 99 Designs, or odesk. Each of these sites has experienced graphic designers who can help you design a professional cover to help sell your book.

The key to getting a great deign is to know what you want before you select a designer. Look at other books in your genre. You don't want to steal anyone else's design, but normally there's a common theme running through many of the book covers. If you find something you like, download that cover so you can send it to your designer. Tell them you like this cover, but you have a few ideas to change it up for your own. You can also send your designer three or four covers that you like to let them know this is the style you're thinking of.

Sometimes I know exactly what I want, and I'll put together a short sketch. Other times, I'll let the designer know I have no idea what I want. When this is the case, I normally have four or five designers create a concept for me. If none of the designs that come back are exactly what I'm looking for I'll try again. Sometimes I might like different portions of several covers, and I'll have one of the designers put it all together for me.

Most recently, I've been more concerned about controlling the images used on my book covers. Some designers on Fiverr have an upcharge to purchase clipart for you, but you never know. If they grab a piece of art without the proper license, it's your butt that's on the line for a lawsuit. Another issue I've run into is I don't remember which designer I used to make some of my earlier covers. This creates problems when I release audio books and paperbacks, because I don't know where to purchase clipart rights for the newer versions of those covers.

Because of this I've begun sourcing most of the clipart for my covers myself before giving the project to a designer. This way I know I'm legal and hold the proper licenses for all of the art work used on my covers. I get most of my clipart from Can Stock Photo, http://www.canstockphoto.com/. Their prices are reasonable and range from $2.50 to $10.00 per use.

I don't claim to be a lawyer or anything, but keep in mind, you need to pay each time you use a piece of clipart. So if your book is available as an eBook, paperback, and audio book, you need to purchase the rights to the clipart three separate times.

After I've picked out the images to use, I put together specific instructions for the cover designer.

I would like a book cover for an Audible audio book. The cover size is 2500 x 2500 pixels. It needs to be a perfect square, and all of the text and images need to be fitted to it. You cannot stretch out the original book cover to fit the space. They will reject the cover.

I am enclosing the original clipart, and a copy of the original book cover. Please keep as close to the original design as possible.

Be sure to specify the exact cover size. Even when you're ordering an eBook cover, every designer seems to deliver it in slightly different dimensions. When you order a Create Space cover, make sure you let the designer know it needs to be delivered as a .pdf file, and that it needs to conform to the Create Space sizing guidelines. I've had several designers deliver the paperback cover as a jpeg, and as a result it was unusable.

If you're ordering a paperback cover for Create Space you need to specify the trim size (example: 6 x 9), the paper style (cream or white), the page style (black and white or color), and how many pages are in your book. Your designer requires all of this information to properly size your cover. You will also need to supply any text or illustrations for the back cover blurb. If you want printing on the spine you need to specify the text.

FYI: Your book needs to be at least 120 pages to have room for a printed message on the spine.

If you're not sure about your cover or your book concept, it can be a good idea to have several covers ready to go.

That way if your book gets off to a slow start you can switch covers and see which one does a better job.

Write a compelling book description. Congratulations. You've done it. You've written an awesome title. You created a dazzling book cover. Now you've just got to close the deal.

How do you turn browsers into buyers?

A compelling book description can get readers drooling for more.

There's no right or wrong way to write a book description.

Some authors start off by asking a question. Others present a dilemma either their reader or their main character may find themselves in. Still others summarize their story. Any of these approaches can work.

What you want to do is draw readers in. Get them hooked on your story, or in the case of nonfiction, on the solution you're presenting. Make it interesting. Create suspense. Make sure they want to read more.

How do you do that?

Ask questions.

Have you ever wondered what life would be like if you took the other road? The one your parents, teachers, and friends told you would put you on a collision course with the others? What if you veered just a little off course, for just a few minutes? Would it change your destiny forever?

Make your case as an authority figure.

Fifteen years as an eBay Power Seller and Top Rated Seller gives Nick a unique combination of experience and knowledge to guide new and experienced sellers through the maze we call eBay.

Introduce your main character.

Max Power stood at the crossroads of now and forever. If he followed her into the time portal everything behind him would disappear forever. If he took the leap his future was uncertain. All Max knew for sure was the girl had saved his life back on Zeta 9. Now she was offering him a future as uncertain as the Zonderan Divide.

Compare your writing to a famous author.

Reviewers say my writing is a cross between Stephen King and Peter Straub with a touch of Kurt Vonnegut thrown in for comedy relief. Read Death Race 3000, and find out for yourself why the Zombie Jesus challenged the Werewolf Devil. Laugh your ass off. Puke your guts out. Run the full gamut of your emotions. You may never want to read another book again – Ever

Books by Nick Vulich

eBay 2014: Why You're Not Selling Anything on eBay, and What you Can Do About it

Freaking Idiots Guide to Selling on eBay: How Anyone Can Make $100 or More Everyday Selling on eBay

Sell it Online: How to Make Money Selling on eBay, Amazon, Fiverr, & Etsy

How to Make Money Selling Old Books & Magazines on eBay

eBay Subject Matter Expert: 5 Weeks to becoming an eBay
Subject Matter Expert

Indie Authors Toolbox

Audio Books by Nick Vulich

eBay 2014: Why Your Stuff Isn't Selling And What You Can Do About It

Freaking Idiots guide to Selling on eBay: How anyone can make $100 or more everyday selling on eBay

Killing the Presidents: Presidential Assassinations and
Assassination Attempts

Manage Like Abraham Lincoln

www.ingramcontent.com/pod-product-compliance
Lightning Source LLC
Chambersburg PA
CBHW020931180526
45163CB00007B/2967

* 9 7 8 1 4 9 9 3 8 9 7 4 6 *